BROTHER$
BO$$ BROTHER$
BO$$ BROTHER$
BO$$ BROTHER$

This book is dedicated to Us!
The Brown 5 Family, for always being
the example of family, for everyone to see.
We are a team and we live everyday with
a mission to be positive, thankful, and to enjoy life.
We love, inspire, and strive for great things at all times!

Thank you to everyone who supports our works!

In Honor Of Calvin "Kool-Aid" Brown.

One Saturday afternoon, Dad asked his three sons, "What would you boys like to do today?"

Nick Jr., The oldest, said, "Let's go out to eat!"

Khaliq and Kharim, the twins, said, "Let's go to the toy store!"

"Ok, we'll do both, but who's going to pay for it…?" asked Dad.

"You Dad! You have all the money!" the boys answered.

Dad smiled, "You boys are right, but I'm going to teach you some things I have learned so you can start to earn your own money. You must pay very close attention, because this will be an important lesson."

"Yes Sir!" said the boys.

"Mom, would you like to come with us?" the boys asked.
"Maybe next time guys", said Mom.
"I'm going to finish my book and tidy up a little" while you guys are out, have fun!"
@teenmemes4life

They headed to their favorite pizza restaurant.

"We're here!" Dad said as he parked.
"Finally! I'm super hungry!" said Nick Jr.

"After we eat, the next stop is the toy store, and you boys will be able to get whatever you want, but...you must pay me back." The boys looked at each other.

"Really, Dad?" Nick Jr. asked curiously.

"Yes, but I don't mean pay me back with money. I mean pay me back by learning the lesson I will teach." Dad explained.

They found a table and placed their order.
The pizzas arrived, and they ate every bite.

Dad listened as the boys talked about
everything they wanted to buy at the toy store.

"If you boys are done, we can go on to the store now."
Dad said.

"Yes, we're ready,
let's go!" The boys said.

They had the biggest smiles their faces
could hold, they were filled with so much joy!

Toy Store
"Ok, boys, you've got 10 minutes to shop and get whatever you want. On your marks, get set, and gooo!" Dad shouted!

The boys quickly picked out
all the things they wanted.

Before they knew it,
10 minutes had passed,
and the boys' carts were full!

"Time's up, boys!"
Dad announced.

Dad paid for everything,
the boys were so happy
and ready to get home.

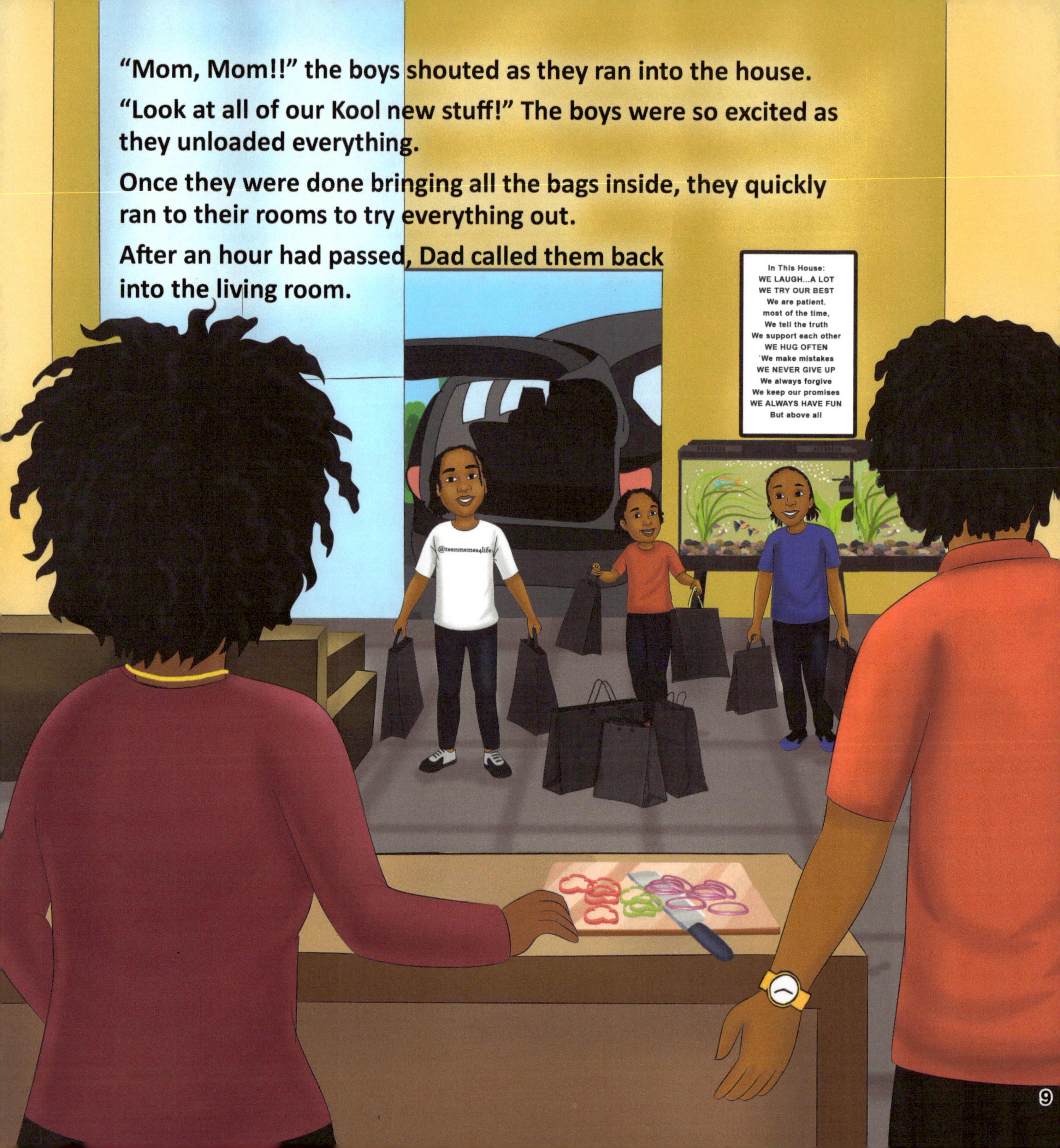

"Mom, Mom!!" the boys shouted as they ran into the house.

"Look at all of our Kool new stuff!" The boys were so excited as they unloaded everything.

Once they were done bringing all the bags inside, they quickly ran to their rooms to try everything out.

After an hour had passed, Dad called them back into the living room.

In This House:
WE LAUGH...A LOT
WE TRY OUR BEST
We are patient.
most of the time,
We tell the truth
We support each other
WE HUG OFTEN
We make mistakes
WE NEVER GIVE UP
We always forgive
We keep our promises
WE ALWAYS HAVE FUN
But above all

Everyone paid attention to hear what Dad had to say.

"Ok boys, the lesson begins with the 4 ways people earn money.

People earn money as employees, self-employed, business owners and as investors.

An employee has a job. Self-employed people work for themselves. Business owners have people who work for them, and investors use money to make more money.

"Dad, why is it so important that we learn this now, we're only children...?" asked Nick Jr.

"I know you boys are children, but it is better to learn this now, instead of having to wait to learn or maybe never learning it at all. It's my job to prepare you boys while you're young, so when you become grown-ups, you'll already know these things, that a lot of people don't know."

The next morning the boys were up early and ready to see what Dad had planned for the day.

"Ok boys, I'm going to start you all off by giving you each a job, which will make you all my what?" Dad asked.

"Employees!" shouted the boys.

"Great job, I see you guys were paying attention." Said Dad.

"Of course we were Dad!" Nick Jr. said.

The boys began as employees washing a few of their neighbors' cars.

By the end of the week, the boys were excited about being able to earn their own money, but they also were exhausted from all the work they had done. They quickly knew that being employees wasn't what they wanted to be long-term.

Dad told the boys that they would earn more money if they continued working together and if they attracted more customers.

Dad took his sons to buy their own car wash supplies with the money they earned from their first week as employees. Dad asked them if they were ready to try the next way people earn money.

They quickly answered, "Yes!"

"We'll be self-employed, so it won't be as hard as the employee!" Nick Jr. said.

"That's true in some ways son, but being self-employed, you own a job, so you still have to do the work." Dad explained.

The boys began the next week as self-employed workers. The word had gotten around, and even more people came to support the boys car wash business. Mom and Dad would watch with pride as the boys greeted and served everyone with respect and a big smile. Things were going very well. However, it was only the 3 of them, so it would sometimes become quite busy.

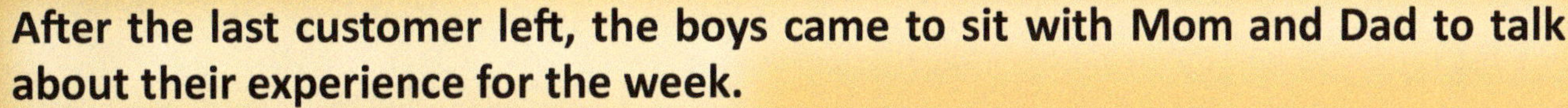

After the last customer left, the boys came to sit with Mom and Dad to talk about their experience for the week.

Nick Jr. spoke for the brothers saying,

"Ok, so, we did last week as employees, this week being self-employed, and now we're ready to have people do the work for us. We need more help Dad!"

"You're right" agreed Dad. "By hiring the right employees and having a system in place, you boys would now be earning money as...?"

"Business owners!" the brothers shouted together.

"That's right," said Dad. "The money that you earn will either be used for assets or spent on liabilities."

"Remember, assets will bring you more money, and liabilities take money away, so you boys must be wise investors with your money."

"You boys must also think of who will best help you run the business." Dad said.

They decided to reach out to a few of their cousins to help.

The brothers liked having employees. It took a lot of pressure away, and they enjoyed the freedom of not having to be the only ones doing all the work.

"I could get used to this." says Nick Jr.

Everything was running smoothly. The boys made almost triple in earnings! They paid their employees, and they paid themselves.

Mom and Dad had made a big purchase for the boys next job as investors. They surprised them with their very own vending machine.

"Kool!" "Whoa!" "Awesome!" the boys shouted with big smiles!

"Once customers start buying the snacks, that money will be used to keep refilling the machine and will also begin to pay you boys." said Mom.

That evening Nick Jr. announced,

"I've got it…BOSS BROTHERS!!!" Nick Jr. shouted with excitement!

"Mom! Dad! That's what we will call our business!"

"Boss Brothers it is then, son." said Dad. "That's a great name!" Mom agreed!

"This is so exciting, we're going to be great Boss Investors just like you Dad!" said Nick Jr.

Dad smiled big! So proud of his sons as they became even better at running the business. They were determined to show Dad that they could do it and all their hard work and effort was all the payback Dad wanted.

The next morning, the "BOSS BROTHERS" business was booming! Cars were washed, and the vending machine was a big hit! Mom and Dad watched their 3 sons in amazement. 3 young businessmen, working together and earning like BOSSES!!!

To Be Continued...

B	B	R	O	T	H	E	R	S	S
U	I	N	L	O	V	E	A	R	E
S	A	G	F	A	M	I	L	Y	L
I	G	T	R	N	I	G	R	G	F
N	R	E	N	S	N	S	E	N	E
E	N	A	A	R	V	N	A	S	M
S	A	M	I	N	E	S	R	S	P
S	G	W	R	G	S	I	N	G	L
O	I	O	G	A	T	G	I	R	O
W	N	R	I	I	O	A	N	S	Y
N	R	K	A	N	R	R	G	N	E
E	E	M	P	L	O	Y	E	E	D
R	L	E	A	R	N	I	N	G	N